DK READERS

Level 2

Level 3

A Note to Parents

DK READERS is a compelling program for beginning readers, designed in conjunction with leading literacy experts, including Dr. Linda Gambrell, Professor of Education at Clemson University. Dr. Gambrell has served as President of the National Reading Conference and the College Reading Association, and has recently been elected to serve as President of the International Reading Association.

Beautiful illustrations and superb full-color photographs combine with engaging, easy-to-read stories to offer a fresh approach to each subject in the series. Each DK READER is guaranteed to capture a child's interest while developing his or her reading skills, general knowledge, and love of reading.

The five levels of DK READERS are aimed at different reading abilities, enabling you to choose the books that are exactly right for your child:

Pre-level 1: Learning to read
Level 1: Beginning to read
Level 2: Beginning to read alone
Level 3: Reading alone
Level 4: Proficient readers

The "normal" age at which a child begins to read can be anywhere from three to eight years old, so these levels are only a general guideline.

No matter which level you select, you can be sure that you are helping your child learn to read, then read to learn!

DK

LONDON, NEW YORK, MUNICH,
MELBOURNE, AND DELHI

Series Editors Deborah Lock and
Penny Smith
U.S. Editor John Searcy
Art Editor Sonia Moore
DTP Designer Almudena Díaz
Production Angela Graef
Jacket Designer Sonia Moore
Photographer Andy Crawford

Reading Consultant
Linda Gambrell, Ph.D.

First American Edition, 2006
06 07 08 09 10 10 9 8 7 6 5 4 3 2 1
Published in the United States by DK Publishing, Inc.
375 Hudson Street, New York, New York 10014

Published in Great Britain by Dorling Kindersley Limited

DK book are available at special discounts for bulk purchases for sales
promotions, premiums, fundraising, or educational use.
For details, contact:
DK Publishing Special Markets
375 Hudson Street
New York, New York 10014
SpecialSales@dk.com

Library of Congress Cataloging-in-Publication Data
Garrett, Leslie, 1964-
 Earth smart--how to take care of the environment / written by Leslie Garrett.--
1st American ed.
 p. cm. -- (DK readers. 2, Beginning to read alone)
Includes index.
ISBN-13: 978-0-7566-1912-1   ISBN-10: 0-7566-1912-2 (pb) --
ISBN-13: 978-0-7566-1913-8   ISBN-10: 0-7566-1913-0 (hb)
 1. Environmentalism--Juvenile literature. I. Title. II. Dorling Kindersley readers.
2, Beginning to read alone.
 GE195.5.G367 2006
 333.72--dc22
                                2005032706

Color reproduction by Colourscan, Singapore
Printed and bound in China by L. Rex Printing Co., Ltd.

The publisher would like to thank the following for their kind
permission to reproduce their photographs:
Position key: a-above; b-below/bottom; c-center; l-left; r-right; t-top
Alamy Images: Ace Stock Ltd. 2tr, 15t; Roger Bamber 32tl; Nigel Cattlin /
Holt Studios International Ltd 27t; David R. Frazier Photolibrary, Inc. 2cr, 17c;
Dennis MacDonald 8c, 10c; Mike Perry 2br, 9br; Anthony Pletts 31b;
Helene Rogers 13br; **Corbis:** 32bl; Louis K. Meisel Gallery 22-23c; Jose Luis
Pelaez, Inc 32br; Guenter Rossenbach / Zefa 32cr; Zefa 13tl; **Ecoscene:**
Jim Winkley 33br; **Getty Images:** Daryl Balfour 19tr; Altrendo Panoramic
18-19b; Mario Lalich / Photonica 4-5c; David Rosenberg 28-29c;
Photographersdirect.com: Jim Kirkikis 25c

With thanks to Mark Jackson for the use of his house, and
to the models: Adam Streamer from Scallywags Agency Ltd.,
Cheryl and Heather Akers.
All other images © Dorling Kindersley
For more information see: www.dkimages.com

Discover more at

www.dk.com

Earth Smart

How to Take Care of the Environment

Written by Leslie Garrett

DK

DK Publishing, Inc.

"Hooray!" shouted Spencer.
"Aunt Charlotte brought us
popsicles!"
Aunt Charlotte was looking after
Spencer and his older sister, Sophie,
for the day.

Aunt Charlotte is a teacher.
Her classes are about the
environment—the world around us.
"We can all take good care
of the environment," she told
the children.

Aunt Charlotte gave
Sophie and Spencer
their popsicles.
Spencer tore off
the wrapper
and tossed it
on the ground.

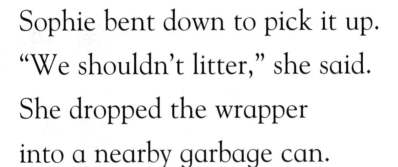

Sophie bent down to pick it up.
"We shouldn't litter," she said.
She dropped the wrapper
into a nearby garbage can.

Put a lid on it
Keep your environment clean
by putting litter in a garbage
can or taking it home. Keep
a lid on your can at home
so garbage doesn't blow away.

Aunt Charlotte agreed: "We need to keep our planet clean so it's a healthy place to live."

Just then a garbage truck
stopped at the curb.
A man emptied the garbage can
into the back of the truck.

"Where is he taking
the garbage?" asked Spencer.
"It goes to a landfill," said
Aunt Charlotte.
"That's a huge pit in the ground
where garbage is dumped, then
covered over with earth.
After a long time, the garbage
breaks down and becomes dirt."

Landfill site
Garbage is spread
out and covered
with earth to keep
flies away and cut
down on smell.

"We should be careful about
the garbage we throw out,"
said Aunt Charlotte.
"Some things are toxic."
"What's toxic?" asked Spencer.

"Things like cans of paint and batteries leak out dangerous chemicals that can get into our soil and water," replied Aunt Charlotte.

Leaking batteries

"If you have dangerous trash like this, get your parents to take it to a hazardous waste drop-off center, where it will be disposed of safely."

Batteries

You will throw away fewer batteries if you use rechargeable batteries or wind-up radios and flashlights.

Turning the handle charges the radio.

The children followed
Aunt Charlotte into the house.
"We throw away too much,"
Aunt Charlotte continued.
"We should recycle as
much as we can.

Drink cans

Aluminum cans
can be recycled over
and over again.
The metal always stays
strong and flexible.

That means saving things
like glass bottles,
plastic food wrappers,
and cans, so they can be
reused or melted down
and turned into
something else."

*A vase made from
recycled glass*

"Let's set up recycling boxes,"
said Sophie.
She found three big boxes
and stuck labels on that said
"paper," "plastic," and
"glass and cans."

Recycling bins

If your recycling boxes are not collected, you can empty them into recycling bins at a local drop-off point.

Spencer found some old newspapers his mother was going to throw away.

He put them in the "paper" recycling box.

"Another way to help our planet
is to save electricity,"
said Aunt Charlotte.
"Power plants burn fuel
to make electricity," she said.
"Smoke from the burning fuel
makes the air dirty."
Spencer coughed.
"We breathe the pollution,"
he said.
"Without clean air, we get sick,"
said Sophie.
Aunt Charlotte nodded.
"And so can our planet," she said.

"The pollution in the air traps heat and makes the planet heat up," explained Aunt Charlotte. "This is called global warming. Ice is melting at both the North and South Poles.

Melting snow
Global warming is making snow melt on Africa's tallest mountain, Mount Kilimanjaro.

This means there will be more floods, and people and animals will lose their homes."

"If we use less electricity,
we will make less pollution,"
said Aunt Charlotte.
"Do you know how we can
use less at home?" she asked.
"We can turn off lights when
we don't need them," suggested
Spencer, as he turned off a light.

"We can read
books instead of
watching TV,"
added Sophie.
The TV was on,
so Sophie
turned it off.

Later they all set out for the park. "Phew," said Spencer as they walked beside a busy road. "What's that smell?"

"That's exhaust from the car engines," said Aunt Charlotte. "It pollutes the air."
"If we walk, we'll cut down on pollution," Sophie suggested.
Aunt Charlotte nodded.

They arrived at the park and
found a place to have a picnic.
"I like the plants and trees in
the park," said Sophie.
"Trees protect us from
air pollution," said Aunt Charlotte.
"They give off oxygen, which
we can breathe.
Trees and other plants make

 the air
healthier.
They also
provide homes
for many kinds
of animals."

They opened a bag of strawberries.
"These are from your uncle's farm,"
Aunt Charlotte said.
"He grows them organically.
That means he doesn't use
chemicals that
can harm the
environment."

Pricey produce

Growing crops using chemicals is easier than growing them organically, so organic food costs more.

"Is that why they're so sweet?" asked Sophie.

"Probably," laughed Aunt Charlotte. "He sells them at the local farmer's market. Since he doesn't travel far, he doesn't create much pollution."

On the way home,
Aunt Charlotte and the children
stopped at the grocery store.
They had to buy food for dinner.

"Let's choose food that's grown nearby," said Aunt Charlotte. They checked the labels to find food grown as close as possible to their town. They found beans, potatoes, chicken, and yogurt for dessert.

As they went home, Sophie said, "Thanks for teaching us to take care of the planet, Aunt Charlotte. Now we can help cut down on pollution."

"And recycle," her aunt added. Spencer picked a chewing-gum wrapper off the ground.

"And I won't litter!" he said.

Save the environment

Remember the four Rs: **Reduce** the amount of things we use so that there's less to throw away, **reuse** things, **recycle** things to make new things, and **rethink** what we buy and use. These horse sculptures have been made from recycled materials.

Litter does not just make a place look ugly. It can also be dangerous to animals and people. It can cause fires and is expensive to clean up.

Natural sources, such as the sun, wind, and waves, can provide us with energy. They can produce heat and electricity without creating pollution.

Trees provide us with better air quality, shelter us from the weather, and attract birds and wildlife. By planting trees, we can have a healthier environment.

Index